Quietly Sitting

ELINOR JONES

GREEN HILL PUBLICATIONS

Front cover artwork © E H McIntyre

ISBN: 0 9521235 6 8

Printed by:
ProPrint
Riverside Cottages
Old Great North Road
Stibbington
Cambs. PE8 6LR

INTRODUCTION

We live in a noisy age of high speed 'everything', from fast food to fast cars, so it is heartening to know that some folks are still drawn to the quiet pursuit of reading poetry, especially that which reflects Christian values. Thank you for choosing this selection which I hope you will find pleasing. The majority of poems are new but I have also included one or two others which appeared in previous publications and were of particular help to some readers.

'Quietly Sitting', the very saying of these words brings a sense of calm. 'Quietly Sitting', a gentle title yet behind it lies a powerful, searching question - how often am *I* found sitting quietly? 'Quietly Sitting' - promise yourself that you'll do it soon and when you do, perhaps you will take this little book with you. May God bless you as you read.

Elinor Jones

PREVIOUS PUBLICATIONS

Green Hill
Publications

**Offering a variety of uplifting literature
including booklets on how to cope as
well as prayer and poetry books**

Quietly Sitting

New for 2003 a collection of
thought-provoking poems to be
read in moments of quietness

£3.00

When God Speaks

A book of deeply personal
prayers covering a wide
variety of life situations.

£2.00 each or 3 for £5.00

Coping With Illness

Words of encouragement,
comfort, and inspiration
for patients in hospital or
at home.

£1.50 each or mix of 3 for £3

COPING WITH LOSS

A helpful booklet for those
who are in the early pangs
of grief.
£1.50 each or mix of 3 for £3

COPING WITH FORGIVENESS

For those who wrestle with
the difficulty of forgiving
those who have hurt them.
£1.50 each or mix of 3 for £3

==========================

Orders to:
Green Hill Publications *
7 Huntburn Ave., Linlithgow
West Lothian EH49 7LE

	No. of Copies	Price
Quietly Sitting		
When God Speaks...................................		
Coping with Illness..............................		
Coping with Loss................................		
Coping with Forgiveness........................		
	Total £	

Cheques payable to: Elinor Jones *
A small donation for P+P
would be appreciated.

CONTENTS

Christmas/New Year

SILENT PRAYER

The country church bestows its peace
As often little churches do
And visitors from far and near
Find respite as they 'take a pew';
They come to lay aside all care,
To rest awhile in silent prayer.

In peaceful yard no sound is heard
As gravestones mark life's shortest span,
And wisest thought cannot prolong
The length of days as given to man;
It's folly to deny God's care,
So come to Him in silent prayer.

When turning to the world again
Let not its rush dictate your pace
But rather let your thoughts return
To God and to this peaceful place;
Cast all into the Master's care,
Who answers every silent prayer.

'Be still and know that I am God.'
                    Psalm 46:10

(St Just in Roseland)

1

FRIENDSHIP

The blessings of friendship
Are warmth and good cheer,
A sure helping hand
And a listening ear;
A shoulder to cry on
When all has gone wrong,
A hearty, 'Well done!'
When success comes along.

Such blessings of friendship
Can also be found
In quiet of evening
When no one's around,
For Jesus is there
And I know it is true,
He's a friend to all those
Who are willing - are you?

HE LISTENS WITH HIS EYES

I see your burden
Let me carry it awhile
My name is Jesus
And I walk the second mile

I see your worries
Lay your head upon my breast
My name is Jesus
Only I can give you rest

I see your heartache
I can feel your throbbing pain
My name is Jesus
Trust in me to bear the strain

I see your weeping
I can hear your listless sighs
My name is Jesus
And I listen with my eyes

I see your weakness
I will give my strength to you
My name is Jesus
Promising to see you through

(Remembering Margaret)

FOLLOWING ON

Alone in the hills I heard my Master's voice
And on that stony path he offered me the choice
Of following no matter where he led
Or pressing on in human strength instead.

Apart from the crowd distractions fell away
Like shadows of the night dispersing with the day
And when all lingering doubtfulness had gone
My mind and heart agreed to follow on.

Along by the stream I felt his presence near
And quietly by the loch his company, so dear,
Brought peace of mind where all the stress had been
To leave me feeling curiously serene.

'Ponder the path of your feet and take
only ways that are firm.'
                                Proverbs 4:26

(Loch Venachar)

DREAMING

Let me dream of youth and heaven,
Dreaming is a soothing balm;
Looking back and looking forward
Brings a sense of calm.

Let me drift in pleasant slumber,
Scenes of youth pass through my mind;
Moving limbs are dancing, running,
Pain is left behind.

Let me glimpse the hope eternal,
In the distance, heaven's gate;
Loving friends and Saviour waiting,
Nothing left to fate.

Let me dream of youth and heaven
While in mortal flesh I stay,
But within life's limitation,
Let me live today.

(For Penny)

CARING

Are you listening, can you hear me,
Are you pulling up a chair?
If I tell you all about me
Will you want to share my care?

Are you looking, do you see me
When your eyes look into mine?
Can you tell my heart is heavy,
Do you read the wordless sign?

Will you do an act of kindness
For this stranger in distress?
Lend an ear and touch my shoulder,
Ease my pain and ease my stress?

If you want to be like Jesus
Stop and think what He would do
If the stranger needing comfort
was no other one but you.

He would listen, really see you,
He would say a little prayer,
He would take the time to comfort,
Always willing to be there.

WHOLESOME LOVE

No hidden motive springs to mind
When Abba beckons me;
No harmful gestures shall I find
While sitting on His knee.
With hands that only move to bless
I know I am secure,
There's healing in His soft caress
For all His ways are pure

He wraps me in a warm embrace,
Enfolds me in His care,
And looking at His gentle face
I find no malice there.
A sense of safety He has brought
Which makes me feel so snug,
The selfless love I long have sought,
Is in God's wholesome hug.

'For you did not receive a spirit that
makes you a slave again to fear, but
you received the Spirit of adoption.
And by him we cry, 'Abba, Father'.
The Spirit himself testifies with our
spirit that we are God's children.'
Romans 8: 15,16

To comfort Jocelyn (real name withheld)

THE CROSS

With callous skill they hammered in the nails
Their only care was not to meet His eye;
Then violently they plunged His cross in place
And left Him there like fish hung out to dry

He slumped, suspended by His hands, His feet,
Twelve stone or more denied not gravity;
The Son of God, the Holy One, and yet
Torn flesh revealed His true humanity

The thoughtful brow that housed the wisest mind
Was pierced with thorns so sharp they thrust within,
And mankind took delight to have His blood
Come streaming down His face and sweat-stained skin

Rough splinters stabbed the rawness of His back
As sounds of laboured breathing filled the air;
His tortured frame grew tense to spare more pain,
Internal organs strained beyond repair

The fiercest pain that man has ever known
Is known to Him whose agonies outweigh
The harshest winds adversity can bring;
All illnesses of youth and of decay

Strong Son of God whose breath was spent for me
Renew my strength, my will to follow on,
I kneel before the Father in Your name
Renouncing sin I come by faith alone

THE CHURCH-YARD IN SPRING

Daffodils, bright in the dappled sunlight
through leafy trees, join cut flowers of
pink and red and gold to lay their colours
against all shades of grey.

Tombstones, neatly arranged, mark the dead.
No trivia spoken here -
such silence is magnificent!

Each bloom, triumphant, nods agreement
to the promise of eternal life.

(St Luke's in Formby)

QUIETLY SITTING

Quietly sitting gazing, raindrops shower the pane
Dimming every colour down the little lane
Green and yellow mingle, rain is hard at play
Sad my lovely daffodils, hang their heads today

Quietly sitting dreaming, tracing sun filled hours
Jewels of rain are forming, light blinks on the flowers
Rain and sun must mingle, both will feed, sustain,
To keep God's garden growing till flowers are born again

Quietly sitting thinking, humans are like flowers
Needing warmth and sunshine, bearing with the showers
Pain and joy must mingle on our earthly road -
In rain as well as sunshine let's trust the hand of God.

'Trust in the Lord with all your heart and lean not on
your own understanding; in all your ways acknowledge
him and he will make your paths straight.'

Proverbs 3:5

RE-CREATION

When green grass grows it always owes
Its richness to the rain
Like seeds of faith that flourish
In the life that suffers pain.

When golden leaves fall to the ground
Fresh buds await the Spring
Like those who bear the longest ills
And wait again to sing.

When crushed, the petals of a rose
Will let a fragrance rise
Like those who triumph over pain
To find a heavenly prize.

When Jesus died and rose again
He offered nail-scarred hands
To show the sick and suffering
He truly understands.

When discontented may I see
Creation's lovely way
And hope, that springs eternal,
Bearing weariness away.

'Be patient then . . . until the Lord's coming,
See how the farmer waits for the land to
yield its valuable crop and how patient he
is for the autumn and spring rains. You too,
be patient and stand firm.'

James 5: 7,8

11

SKYWARD

Blankets of purple thrown over the hills
Sun-kissed the loch down below
Stony the pathway that leads to the top
Yet onward and upward I go

Up where the silence erases all strain
My thoughts are unfettered and free
Nothing disturbing my innermost self
And peace lays her stillness on me

AS ONE

Thank You, Lord, for fellowship
With those who seek your face:
Thank You too it matters not
Their school, their church, their race,
For in the bond of Jesus
Such things have little sway
And we forget our differences
When hearts unite to pray.

Thank You, Lord, you made each one
To vary from the rest;
Thank You too for holding back
From saying who is best
For just like little snowflakes
No two are quite the same
Yet each, when joined with others, shall
Your handiwork proclaim.

Thank you, Lord, for giving us
The Way, the Truth, the Life
Thank You too for harmony
Transcending earthly strife.
For through Your Holy Spirit
And the gift of Christ Your Son
All barriers are broken down
And praise ascends as one.

(For believers everywhere)

IN HIS SERVICE

Praise the Lord, you joyful Christians,
Give Him glory, lift His Name;
Let the love of God inspire you
And His ways proclaim.

Thank the Lord, you grateful Christians
For His coming down to earth
With the plan of His salvation,
Bringing us re-birth.

Bless the Lord, you prayerful Christians,
Come to Him on bended knee;
Touch the hands that safely keep you
And the nail-prints see.

Serve the Lord, you willing Christians,
Feed the hungry, clothe the poor;
Pray with those whose hearts are heavy,
Jesus has the cure!

Love the Lord, you faithful Christians,
Work with Jesus, freely give;
Praise and thank and bless and serve Him
By the way you live.

PURE WORSHIP

In quietness the Spirit came
To touch, with stillness, every heart;
As silent lips proclaimed Him Lord
He bid all evil things depart.

With reverence sweet, before our God,
Each one released all selfish thought
And, one in spirit, gently said
The lovely prayer that Jesus taught.

In worship free of self and sin
The very room was filled with light;
His gentle love caressed each mind,
For all was pleasing in His sight.

'Our Father, in heaven, hallowed
be Your name'
                              Matthew 6:9

IT'S YOUR LOVE

Refrain
It's your love that draws me to you,
It's your love, it's your love;
All forgiving tender Father
It's your love, it's your love.

Verse
Even when I was a stranger
To the truth that you were there
Love stood vigil all around me
Till I wakened to your care.

Refrain
Though with sin my life is tainted
Day to day and year to year
Touched by love I come confessing,
In your presence, feel no fear.

Refrain
When at last I leave this body
All my sin will melt away
And rejoicing in my Saviour
I shall sing on that great day

Refrain
It's your love that draws me to you,
It's your love, it's your love;
All forgiving tender Father
It's your love, it's your love.

REACTIONS

Retaliation, the natural instinct
when wronged, when hurt.
Retaliation, a sweet revenge
For hatred, for violence
And all the lesser wrongs of . . .
bitter words, unkind gossip,
twisted truth, unkept promises.

Retaliation, fleeting rough justice
To ease the pain
To settle the account.

Forgiveness, the unnatural reaction
When wronged, when hurt.
Forgiveness, a sweet response
To quell hate's flow
To calm the strife
To stem all bitterness
Refining Nature's sway . . .
In ways of peace
In ways of care
In ways of love
In ways of God.

Forgiveness, undeserved love,
Easing the pain
Settling the account.

CHANGE ME

Empty my life of selfishness,
Take away pettiness too,
Erasing the stains of childishness
That mar my walk with You.

Empty my mind of churlishness,
Take away envy and pride,
Sweeping aside all unpleasantness
That makes me sour inside.

Empty my soul of ugliness,
Take away canker and taint,
Changing my ways into loveliness
Becoming of a saint.

INNER BEAUTY

As age or illness bears my strength away
And I depend on others for my care
Let graciousness become my outer way,
My inner thoughts protect from selfish snare.

Refine in me the life that still remains,
Let earthly things release their fleeting charms;
May I recall that God alone sustains
And underneath are everlasting arms.

When weakness overwhelms or hope recedes
Anxiety would steal my inner calm
Yet I remember Jesus intercedes
And righteous ones shall flourish like the palm.

May inner beauty shine, though weak my shell,
My trust in God be ever clearly seen;
Let faith abound, my lips be quick to tell
That Jesus keeps my spirit evergreen.

'The righteous will flourish like a palm tree . . .
they will flourish in the courts of God . . .
they will still bear fruit in old age, they will
stay fresh and green, proclaiming, 'The Lord
is upright; he is my Rock'.
                              Psalm 92:12-15

(For older friends . . . and weary friends)

REMEMBRANCE SUNDAY

Dressed in blue with badges gleaming,
We crunched our way in drill-form to the church doors,
Halted in perfect unison and stood erect.
Queen's colours, Guides' colours hung limply,
Responding only to our shivers in the cold November air.

Proudly we carried our flags and dipped them low
Beneath the horse-shoe balcony.
Sharp intakes of breath as a flag-staff skiffed the wood.
Nervous giggles stifled,
We raised our standards, and slow-marched on.

His blood-red poppy softened ministerial black;
His nod, our signal,
And solemnly we presented colours,
Took one pace back and sighed with relief.

Two minutes silence, an eternity for post-war school girls.
Thoughts swarming in the ever-thickening stillness,
The sound of breathing filled our ears.
Try as we might,
How could we remember men we never knew?

Women wept and men pretended not to,
But stiff upper lips quivered at the sound of,
'They shall not grow old
         as we who are left grow old . . .'.
A rhythmic sound, a plaintive sound, a soothing sound,
Though we scarcely knew why.

Dim was our understanding then,
Those faceless heroes, myriad saviours
Died for us, how strange yet wonderful it seemed
To die for those as yet unborn;
Lives sacrificed to break the grip of evil men
That we might live in freedom.
Impressive, yes, but infant eyes saw only symbols;
Uniforms, flags, medals, poppies.

Only now do I fully understand that gift.
The soldier-saviours gave their lives,
Reluctantly, unwittingly, securing our peace.

In adulthood another truth dawns . . .

The Saviour gave His life
Freely, intentionally, securing our souls -
The greatest sacrifice of all.

(Fond thoughts of St Paul's in Leith)

LET US FORGIVE

Why quarrel
For life is but a breath
Why quarrel
How short the years till death;
With sin-stained lips would we meet the Lord
Ashamed of our days of bitter discord

Consider
How Jesus quelled all strife
Consider
His perfect loving life;
With quiet word to all those who came
He gently forgave, let us do the same.

Forgiven,
So now we should forgive.
Forgiven,
A richer way to live;
Our God would have us resemble His Son
In peaceful forgiveness to live at one.

COME CLOSE

Let me come close, Lord, close to Your side
Where in Your presence I may abide
Keep me safe from every harm
Let me lean upon Your arm

Let me come close, Lord, close to Your cross
There let me measure my own soul's loss
Should I e'er Your name deny
Or without You should I die.

Let me come close, Lord, close to Your heart
Beat to its rhythm, never depart
Let Your love be my love too
Keep my heart in tune with You

Let me come close, Lord, close to Your ear
There give assurance You'll gladly hear
Every word I speak in prayer
For all those placed in my care

Let me come close, Lord, close to Your light
Shine in the darkness, grant inner sight
When Your way I long to see
Then, Lord, You'll come close to me.

PASS IT ON

Lord let my words be simple
And always jargon-free
When telling other people
Of the things You do for me

Lord let my deeds be kindly
As from a thankful heart
That others know the blessing
Of the love that You impart

Lord let my life be pleasing
Make plain to all around
The happiness they see in me
In Jesus can be found.

THE POWER OF PRAYER

I prayed with unbelieving friend
And lovely was that prayer,
For doubt and faith began to blend
As Jesus met us there.

We prayed of troubles on the mind,
Of broken heart and dream
We asked that pain be left behind,
For balm where hurt had been.

Then inner peace we quietly found
The peace that comes from God
My friend confirmed with gentle sound
And then with gentle nod.

I sat amazed to see doubt melt
In one who doubted so
And humbled by God's goodness, felt
A deep and thankful glow.

The presence of the Living Lord
Is all our need today
No greater gift to doubting friend
Than teaching her to pray.

Jesus said, 'Where two or three are
gathered together in my Name, there
am I in the midst of them.'
                    Matthew 18:20

(Maria, remembered)

THE FORGOTTEN ONES

Ragged clothes, unshaven face,
Tramp of every city
Huddled in his usual place
Relying on our pity

Toss a coin or pass him by
Frugal our compassion,
Rarely hear his deeper cry
Or feel with honest passion

Busy lives and lack of care
Self instead or others,
Soon forgetting he was there
The least of all our brothers

Cup of water in God's name?
Second coat bestowing?
Soup and comfort to sustain
Is love in action showing?

Prayer and pocket must combine
To prove that we have pity
On tramps who, not by God's design,
Exist in every city

(Edinburgh and other cities)

PARTNERS IN MISSION

They leave home and country to serve you, O Lord,
To take forth the Gospel as urged by your Word:
Inspired by compassion and pictures of need
They go at your bidding to 'sow the good seed'.

They care not for danger, secure in your hand,
And know all their future is carefully planned:
They follow your leading, are mindful in prayer
Wherever they go, take the Lord Jesus there!

They feed hungry souls of the poor and the lost
And give of themselves without counting the cost
They put us to shame by the way that they live
But does their example inspire us to give?

The Lord may not want us to serve in strange lands
But care of those 'strangers' is still in our hands
For we here at home and in spiritual health
Are partners in mission when sharing our wealth.

TO LOVE

Lord, we are *your* people so help us
To appreciate one another
To forgive one another
To love one another.
Only as we learn to love those within our circle
Do we become equipped to love those outwith it.

Grant us a love for those we find unlovable
Remembering that you, O Lord, love them.
Enable us to love in Your power
For our own is so feeble.

Help us
To refine our thoughts
To hold our tongues
To look for good
So that your kind of love
Controls all we say and do.

Save us
From unkind ways
From ungracious attitudes
From hardness of heart

For in loving others
We become true disciples,
In loving others
We find the secret of pleasing You.

'The fruit of the Spirit is . . . love . . . longsuffering,
gentleness . . .'

Galatians 5:22

(At Inverness)

BETHLEHEM HUSH

Come to a place of the long, long ago,
Come to that place now - and there I will show
You a portrait of contrast, of shades dark and light,
Come to the manger this hushed Christmas night.

See how the Census brought folks from afar,
Business was lively and nothing could mar
The trade of the craftsmen, the greed of the crush
but few found their way to the Bethlehem hush.

The women were baking, the men sold their ware,
The noise and the bustle made no one aware
Of the quiet emergence of Jesus our Lord,
Ordained by our Father, the Incarnate Word.

And those, in our cities, two thousand years on
Are buying and selling when they might have gone
To places of quietness away from the rush
To worship the Saviour in Bethlehem's hush.

So come to a place of the long, long ago,
Yes, come to that place if your longing to know
If Jesus still lives, on this hushed Christmas Eve;
He does - when you open your heart and believe.

CHRISTMAS JOY

In the lamp-light of the stable
Shepherds hearts began to glow,
Kindled by that warmth of Jesus
Only true believers know.

Deep the joy that welled within them
For the Gift that God had sent,
Greatest scribe could never pen their
Wordless praise, so eloquent.

Silently with them we worship
As our hearts and minds we raise
Till at last our lips, unfastened,
Break forth into songs of praise.

ETERNAL LOVE

From infant cry to dying hour
The love of God envelops me;
It warms the course of earthly life,
It promises eternity.

This love is not as other loves
As precious as these loves may be;
While passions fade and elders pass
God loves me to eternity.

Dear Lord, Redeemer, clothed in flesh
The heart of Christmas mystery;
By faith Your timeless love is mine
Both now and for eternity.

'Your throne was established long ago;
you are from all eternity.'
                              Psalm 93:2

AFTER CHRISTMAS

Christmas joy now faded like the tree,
Needle-bare disowning former glee;
Lights switched off all neatly stowed away
Faith now boxed until next festive day.

Christmas gifts yet none could satisfy,
Empty souls left crying, parched and dry;
Untouched hearts can find no song to sing,
Distant bells still echo, hollow ring.

Christmas gone, it's fleeting joys recede,
Weary souls are bruised with aching need:
Time ticks on and whispers, 'It's too late . . .'
Jesus shows an ever-open gate!

Christmas Child shine now your timeless light,
Break upon the soul's long winter night;
Open gate receiving sinners still
Enter now, it is the Father's will.

'Now is the time of God's favour,
now is the day of salvation.'
2 Corinthians 6:2

IN FAITH

A fresh New Year lies silently ahead,
No footprints yet across untrodden snow
And wandering feet are waiting to be led
By One who knows the pathway down below:
So I in faith shall step I know not where
And give, in trust, to Him my everything,
For God, my Guide, Protector, will be there
Long after sun-kissed snow gives way to Spring.

'Show me your ways, O Lord, teach me your
paths: guide me in your truth and teach me,
for you are God my Saviour, and my hope is
in you all day long.'

Psalm 25:4,5